Wood

Edited by Rebecca Stefoff

Text © 1991 by Garrett Educational Corporation

First Published in the United States in 1991
by Garrett Educational Corporation,
130 East 13th, Ada, Oklahoma 74820

First Published in 1989 by A & C Black (Publishers) Limited, London
with the title WOOD
© 1989 A & C Black (Publishers) Ltd.

Manufactured in the United States of America

Library of Congress Cataloging in Publication Data

Jennings, Terry J.
    Wood / Terry Jennings.
    p. cm.—(Threads)
    Summary: Discusses the origin and processing of wood, its uses, and
the need to protect trees.
    ISBN 1-56074-002-7 : $15.93
    1. Wood—Juvenile literature.   2. Wood products—Juvenile literature.
[1. Wood.] I. Title. II. Series.
SD541.J46 1991
674—dc20
                                      91-18187
                                          CIP
                                          AC

Wood

Terry Jennings

Photographs by Ed Barber

Contents

GEC **GARRETT EDUCATIONAL CORPORATION**

How do you use wood?

Wood is one of our most important materials. It's used for making lots of different things, from houses and boats to pencils and matches. The paper for this book was made from wood. Have a look around your school or home. Where can you see wood being used?

Looking at wood

Make a collection of wooden objects and small pieces of wood. Try to find several different kinds of wood. A carpenter or a builder may let you have some spare pieces of wood. Perhaps you can find some in the woods or in the park.

In your collection, does any of the wood have sharp splinters? If so, be careful of these.

Look closely at the wood you have collected. Use a magnifying glass if you have one. How many differences can you find?

Look at your pieces of wood from the side. Are any of them made up of layers or tiny chips? What does the wood feel like?

Fill a large bowl with water and put your pieces of wood into it, one at a time. Do they float or sink? If they float, do they float high or low in the water?

5

Can you see a pattern on any of your pieces of wood? Wood is made up of lots of long, thin threads called fibers. Sometimes these fibers are straight; sometimes they are wavy or even a spiral shape. The pattern they make is called the "grain" of the wood.

Are there any swirls, or "knots," like these in the wood?

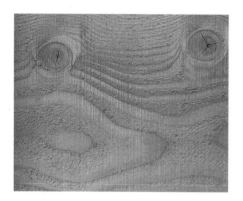

They show where a branch joined the trunk of a tree.

To keep a record of the different patterns made by the grain and the knots, make some wood rubbings. Put a piece of paper on top of the wood and rub over the surface with a crayon. Hold the paper still while you rub.

6

Where does wood come from?

Wood comes mainly from the trunks and branches of trees. The wood is underneath the bark, which protects the wood while it is growing. Wood is made up of millions of tiny tubes that carry food and water around inside the tree.

Every year, a tree grows a new layer of wood around the outside of its trunk and branches. This layer is called an annual ring — annual means "yearly." If you count all the annual rings in the trunk of a cut tree, you can tell how old the tree was. Can you work out the age of the pine tree in this photograph?

Each kind of tree has a different sort of wood. There are two main groups of trees, which are called "hardwoods" and "softwoods."

The names do not always mean that the wood is soft or hard. The real difference is that hardwoods are trees with broad leaves that fall off the tree in winter. Softwoods are trees that have their seeds in cones. Most of them have needle-like leaves that stay on the tree all year round. Hardwoods grow very slowly, and softwoods grow more quickly.

Which of these trees do you think are hardwoods? Which do you think are softwoods? (The answers are on page 25.)

Growing wood

oftwood trees, such as pine or
ruce, are planted in large forests
lled plantations. When the trees
e fully grown, they are cut down
 that their wood can be used;
ew young trees are planted to
ke their place.

he young trees grow from seeds
at are planted in places called
urseries. The tractors above are
lanting seeds from spruce trees.

 a year or two, the tiny trees are
ug up and moved to land nearby.
ere they have more room to grow
ntil they are big enough to be
lanted out in the forest.

Would you like to grow your own forest?

You will need

Damp soil or potting compost

Flower pots

Some water

Tree fruits and seeds

How to do it

1. Fill the flower pots with the damp soil or potting compost. With your finger, make a small hole in the top of the soil and drop one seed into each pot. Cover the fruits or seeds with some more soil and pat down the soil gently.

2. Put the pots on a sunny windowsill. If you keep the pots warm and moist, the fruits and seeds will start to grow roots and leaves. Be patient, because it may take a long time.

Cutting down trees

The people who cut down trees are called lumberjacks. They use special power saws called chain-saws, and they can make a tree fall exactly where they want it to. This lumberjack is cutting down a fir tree.

Once the tree has been cut down, the lumberjack cuts off the branches. Then a large machine picks up the logs and stacks them in big piles.

The next job is to cut the logs into planks. This takes place in a sawmill. In some countries, the logs are floated down a river to reach the sawmill. But most logs are carried on trucks or special trains.

When the logs arrive at the sawmill, they are stacked in large heaps. A truck lifts a few logs at a time and takes them into a building where machines cut up the logs.

These oak logs will be made into fence posts.

1. First, each log is sawn into thin slices with a band-saw.

2. The slices cut by the band-saw move on rollers to a different sawing machine.

3. Here a re-saw cuts up the slices into narrow strips.

4. Finally, a cross-cut-saw trims the ends off each narrow strip. The wood is then ready to use for fence posts.

Drying wood

Wood that has just been cut in a sawmill contains a lot of water. It usually has to be dried, or seasoned before it can be used. The seasoning makes the wood harder and stiffer it keeps its shape better.

Sometimes the wood is left to dry in the air. The planks have to be stacked in a special way. Little sticks keep the planks apart, so that air can blow between them. These oak planks will be left to dry for several years.

It's much quicker to dry wood in a large oven called a kiln. Warm air is blown through the planks to help the wood to dry. The planks are left in the kiln for about 7-10 days.

How strong is wood?

After the wood has been seasoned, it is ready to be smoothed, sawed, or cut into different shapes and sizes.

A lot of wood is used when a house is built. In the picture, can you see how much wood goes into the roof of a house? Wood is used in the roofs of houses because it is strong but light.

Try this test to see how strong wood is

You will need

Heavy weights (such as bricks)

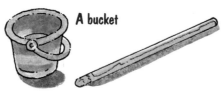

A bucket

A narrow strip of wood (dowel is about right)

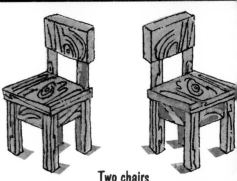

Two chairs

How to do it

Hang an empty plastic bucket from the middle of the strip of wood and rest the wood between the two chairs. Make sure your toes are not under the bucket and then put the weights into the bucket one at a time.

How many weights can you add before the wood breaks?

15

Shaping wood

Wood can also be carved and shaped. This man is making a guitar. He is using a tool called a plane to smooth the wood.

Sometimes pieces of wood are worn and shaped by the sea. This is called driftwood. If you visit the seaside, collect pieces of driftwood that are an unusual shape. Rub the pieces of wood with sandpaper to make them smooth. You may like to varnish your wooden shapes; ask an adult to help you with this.

16

Different kinds of wood

Veneers

Some logs have a beautiful grain which makes them very valuable. Many of these logs are cut into thin slices called veneers. The log is turned against a sharp blade, like this, and then cut into rectangles.

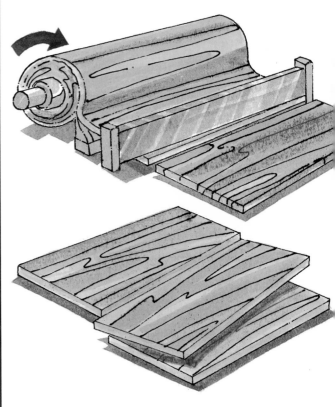

The veneer is then glued over plainer pieces of wood. If you look at the edges of doors or drawers, you can often see the edge of the layer of veneer.

~ywood, blockboard,
~d particleboard

~wood is made by gluing thin sheets of
~od together. The sheets are made from
~s in the same way as veneers.

~ckboard is rather like a sandwich
~de of strips of wood.

~ticleboard is made from small pieces
~wood and sawdust that are glued
~ether in big sheets.

~ould you like to try
~king your own particleboard?

~u will need

A matchbox

A spoon

A bowl

Some glue
or wallpaper paste

Sawdust
(you can buy this
from a pet shop)

~w to do it

~ a little sawdust and some glue or paste
~ the bowl. Stir with the spoon to make
~icky mixture and pour this mixture into
~ matchbox. When the mixture is dry,
~l off the matchbox.

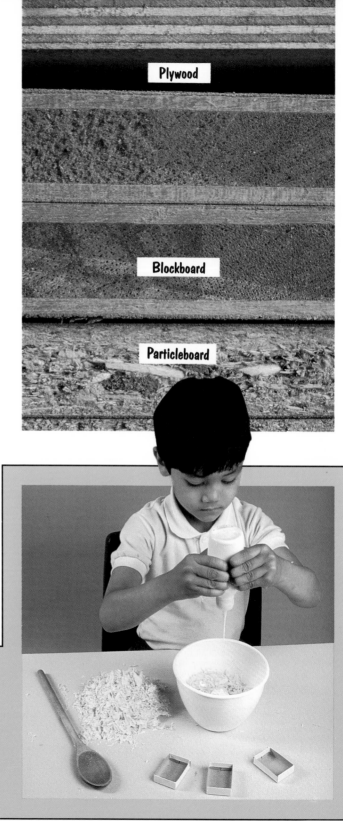

Plywood

Blockboard

Particleboard

Wood and paper

Even small logs are useful. Many of them are made into wood pulp. The bark is taken off the logs and they are then chopped up into tiny chips, like the ones in the picture. The wood chips are ground up or mixed with chemicals to make a wet, mushy pulp.

Most wood pulp is turned into paper.

can turn paper back into the wood fibers it was made from
making papier mâché. The words mean "paper pulp."

u will need

An old spoon

Some flour

A bucket
of water

Newspaper or tissues

A cup

w to do it

Tear up old newspapers or tissues into small pieces. Put a little
ur into a cup and stir in enough water to make a thick paste.

2. Mix the paste into a
ucket of water and
hen stir the pieces of
aper into the liquid.

3. After a few hours,
ou will have a pulpy
ass of fibers.
queeze the water
ut of the pulp and
old it into the
hape you want.
imple shapes such
s owls or people's
eads are easiest
o make.

Leave the shapes to dry in a warm place. In a few
s, they will be almost as hard as the wood that the
rs came from in the first place.

Charcoal

Charcoal is one of the most useful substances made from wood. It is made by partly burning small logs in a special oven, like the one in the picture. In this sort of oven, the wood burns very slowly.

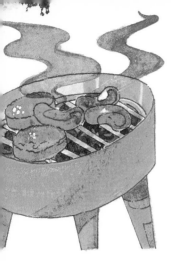

At barbecues, people cook their food on top of burning charcoal. Powdered charcoal is used in the making of fireworks and gunpowder.

Artists often use charcoal for drawing or sketching. Try making your own pictures with charcoal. How is charcoal better than pencil or crayon? In which ways is charcoal less good?

Protecting wood

When trees die, small animals, fungi, and bacteria feed on the wood and make it slowly rot away. The remains of the wood go into the soil where they help other trees and smaller plants to grow.

Find a small rotting log and gently pull the wood apart with your fingers. What does the rotting wood smell like? What does it feel like? Which small animals can you find living in the log? When you have studied the animals, put them back under another rotting log.

The wood used in furniture and buildings will also rot
if it is not protected. Chemicals, such as creosote, can
be brushed on wood that will be used ourdoors. The
creosote stops insects and fungi from eating the wood.
Paints and varnishes keep insects and fungi away and
also make the wood look smooth and shiny.

Save our trees

People are cutting down trees faster than new ones can be planted. In some tropical countries, whole forests of valuable hardwood trees have been cut down. The animals that lived in the forest have nowhere to go. When it rains, the soil is washed away because there are no tree roots to hold it in place. Large areas of softwood trees are also cut down to make paper.

We must plant new trees whenever we can and use wood more carefully. We can also help to save trees by not wasting paper. For every ton of waste paper we collect for recycling, we save 17 trees.

Now you know why wood is such an important material and why we must look after our trees. Next time you use something made from wood, think about the tree it came from.

More things to do

1. Compare the hardness of different small pieces of wood by seeing how easy or difficult it is to drive nails into them. Do any of the pieces of wood split when a nail is driven into them? Which kinds of wood are they?

2. Weigh some small, dry pieces of wood. Soak them in a bowl of water for 48 hours. Take them out, wipe them dry with a cloth or blotting paper. Weigh the pieces of wood again. Which of the pieces have gained the most weight? Put some of your pieces somewhere warm, such as a radiator, to dry out. Watch what happens to the wood as it dries. This is why wood needs to be seasoned.

3. Draw an outline picture on a large sheet of paper. Lightly paint inside the picture with gum or paste. Sprinkle sawdust or wood shavings on the gum or paste to make a collage.

4. Collect several small pieces of the same kind of wood. Try to paint them using a different kind of paint for each piece. Which kinds of paint cover the wood best? If you try this activity with pieces of wood of another kind, do you get the same result?

5. Study a tree in your garden or in the school grounds for a whole year. Keep a diary of what you discover about your tree. What birds and other animals do you see on your tree? How does your tree change from one season to another?

6. Try making your own model of a log raft. Find some twigs and cut them all to the same length. Use cotton thread to tie them together like the ones in the diagram below. Put your log raft on a bowl of water. Does it float? What weight of toy bricks will your raft hold and still stay afloat?

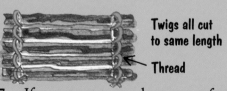

Twigs all cut to same length

Thread

Acorn

Bottles full of water

7. If you want to see larger tree fruits and seeds, such as acorns, start to grow, place them on bottles of water, like this.

Answers to page 8: top left, larch trees (softwood); top right, ash trees (hardwood); bottom, Norway spruce (softwood).

Index

(Numbers in **bold** type are pages that show activities.)